# Enjoying Your Relationship

## First Principles in Marriage

by Jeff Reed

**A six-session Bible study for small groups**

**THE FIRST PRINCIPLES**

SERIES TWO

© LearnCorp Resources, 1998

All rights reserved. No part of this publication may be reproduced, stored in a retrieval system, or transmitted in any form or by any means (electronic, mechanical, photocopy, recording, or any other) except for brief quotations in printed reviews, without the prior permission of the publisher.

LearnCorp Resources is committed to assisting churches, parents, Christian schools, and Christian businessmen and women with resources to carry out their ministries.

These materials are designed to integrate with BILD-International resources, which are designed to help churches train leaders.

Art Direction & Design: Bill Thielker

Background cover image: used by permission of Standard Publishing Company, Cincinnati, Ohio.

All Scripture, unless otherwise noted, is from the New American Standard Bible.

ISBN 1-891441-04-3

# Table of Contents

# PREFACE – A Living Story

This series has grown out of the labor of many faithful believers. It has been developed in the context of the ministry of establishing churches for over 25 years. The story of its development is truly a living story, filled with faithful men and women serving Jesus Christ as they build their lives, families, and churches upon these first principles.

A first word of thanks goes to my immediate family. To my wife, Nancy, who has taught me the true meaning of faithfulness. To the editing team, which is made up of the three generations of women in my life–Nancy, my mother-in-law Maxine, and my daughter Anna–whose lives truly adorn the gospel. Without this team, the booklets would not be grammatically correct or readable. In addition, thanks to my son Jonathan, who is diligently laboring to make this series live for high school students, and to my son-in-law George Stagg, who has overseen the entire publishing project. Both are emerging as faithful, young ministers of the gospel.

A word of thanks to my church family–Ontario Bible Church–who have endured the endless development of this material over the 25 years, beginning with ugly green notebooks. This small, faithful group of believers have built their lives on the first principles of the faith and are now reaping the fruit of their labor in the lives of their children and in a worldwide ministry.

A word of thanks to all the leaders and churches who are part of BILD International's worldwide network, who have faithfully used and contributed to the development of BILD resources from which this series is developed and in which it is designed to be integrated. Already several translation projects have begun to place this series in other languages. Special thanks to Don McReavy, who goaded me into producing the initial *Establishing Series*, and who continues to labor with me in its development.

A word of thanks to my two partners in LearnCorp Resources–Bob Goris and Charlie Stagg. Just as many strategic people helped make the apostle Paul's journeys possible, they have invested significant resources to make this series a reality. In addition, thanks to Bill Thielker, an outstanding designer, who truly seeks to be faithful to the skills and craft that God has entrusted to him.

On behalf of the entire church family listed above, it is our prayer that God will use this series as a modern day didache–or catechism if you will–to help establish tens of thousands, if not hundreds of thousands, in the first principles of the faith, that their churches might multiply and their families produce fruit for generations to come.

Jeff Reed

October, 1997

# ENJOYING YOUR RELATIONSHIP—Introduction

The marriage relationship is being radically redefined. In our postmodern culture, it includes redefining the essence of manhood and womanhood. Each person is on his or her own enlightened journey to become all that he or she can be rather than putting the family and its responsibilities first. Individual preference has become primary. The traditional family is under attack. Leadership and authority have been eroded.

This change has been underway for several decades now, and it is global in nature. Because we live in a global village, the changes in the West are having an almost instant impact on many of the developing countries.

In light of the ideological battle of these global realities, the title, *Enjoying Your Relationship,* might seem a bit trivial. We all desire to have an enjoyable marriage relationship. However, in light of the postmodern redefinition of marriage and the pressing practical question in our Western culture of whether a contemporary marriage relationship can even survive for a lifetime, wouldn't a more sophisticated title be in order? Today, we know that less than 60% of all marriages in the USA will survive, let alone flower into satisfying and enjoyable relationships. All of us have experienced the effects of this ideological change. We all know someone who has experienced a divorce, probably someone in our extended, if not immediate, families. We have concerns for our children. Will they enjoy satisfying, lifelong relationships? If you live in a traditional culture, you may have concerns that your culture will tread the same path. You may even have concerns for your own relationship. For many, this concern may be part of what has brought them to Christ.

What does all of this have to do with the first principles of the faith? Both the marriage relationship and family life lie at the very center of the first principles. At first, Christian guidelines for the marriage relationship may seem archaic, out of touch with contemporary culture. Yet, once we really understand them, we will begin to see God's wisdom. We will begin to understand their beauty and the residual effects that lead to a fruitful heritage, which can produce for generations to come.

We will see that God's design for marriage and the family is not a set of guidelines that take the fun out of it all. (*Puritanical* now has been historically redefined in our culture to mean boring and prudish.) But when properly understood and followed, they will bring a deep and lasting enjoyment into every aspect of marriage and family life.

This series of booklets (Series 2, books 1-4) focuses on the family: first the marriage relationship, then the children, followed by the work of the family unit, and finally, intergenerational heritage issues. Through the process of studying this series, you will learn the core principles for building a lasting, enjoyable marital relationship that produces faith and a heritage in your children; for building a productive, successful family economic unit; and for producing a family that can participate together in building Christ's church.

In this first booklet, *Enjoying Your Relationship,* we will turn our attention to God's design for the marriage relationship. In session one, we will look at the cultural confusion that has come into our churches, upsetting whole families, and why it is critical for families to have guidelines for living within the household of God. In session two, we will begin building a framework for our marriages, examining the essential roles and responsibilities of husbands and wives to each other. In session three, we will look at the heart–or spirit–of a marriage, the emotional glue of the relationship, and how it affects our effectiveness for Christ. In session four, we will look at marriage relationships in the context of community life and the critical role that the local church community plays in building strong marriages. Finally, in session five, we will look at the intergenerational rewards of building lifelong marriages within the context of Christ's plan for the ages.

In one sense, this book is about building enjoyable, rich marriages that span a couple's life together. In another sense, this book is about building strong churches, for strong families are the essence of strong churches. The household guidelines from the New Testament letters are not arbitrary. Our Master designed them, and we are obligated to follow them, as His disciples. So let's begin the process of building strong marriages according to Christ's design.

# THE FIRST PRINCIPLES SERIES

## The Demands of Today's Fast-Paced Society

We are entering a whole new way of life—computers, endless streams of information, new work realities—which demands continuous learning. This environment puts tremendous pressure on our time, finances, and relationships.

As Christians, we are under even more pressure. Besides making a living in this society and doing a good job in our homes and marriages, there is the extra desire to serve God, which includes having an effective ministry. Students have to juggle assignments, work hours, and family involvement, as well as involvement in a local church and the tremendous opportunity for ministry among peers. This involves more time and resources—in our homes, in the workplace, at school, and directly in the lives of our local church communities. There seems to be little time for our own personal growth and development.

Our culture builds into us a mindset about so many things, one of which is our personal development.

We want quick fixes—not long-term solutions.

We want how to's—not the ability to think clearly.

We want short training—not lifelong learning.

We want tantalizing subjects—not serious ordered learning.

We want fill-in-the-blank exercises—not reflective writing.

We want one-time applications—not serious projects.

If we are going to be effective as Christians in the coming century, we must carve out regular time for personal growth and development. This cannot be neglected if we expect significant fruit to come from our lives. We must have some sort of strategy that will help guide us lifelong. And we must take the first step.

*The First Principles Series* is designed to be just such a first step.

# Design of The First Principles Series I-III

This booklet is part of a set of four booklets, which make up Series I. The whole collection, Series I-III, totals thirteen booklets. They are all built around an idea found in Paul's letter to the church at Colossae written almost 2000 years ago.

> See to it that no one takes you captive through philosophy and empty deception, according to the tradition of men, according to the elementary principles of the world, rather than according to Christ. (Colossians 2:8)

The phrase "the elementary principles" is best translated as "the first principles." They are the basic fundamentals of the faith. They represent the first things that must be learned, upon which everything else is built. If they are not carefully understood, everything else will be distorted. The writer of the letter to the Hebrews understood this when he exhorted the Hebrew Christians who were forgetting their newfound faith, in Hebrews 5:

> 11) Concerning him we have much to say, and *it is* hard to explain, since you have become dull of hearing. 12) For though by this time you ought to be teachers, you have need again for someone to teach you the elementary principles of the oracles of God, and you have come to need milk and not solid food. 13) For everyone who partakes only of milk is not accustomed to the word of righteousness, for he is a babe. 14) But solid food is for the mature, who because of practice have their senses trained to discern good and evil.

The Hebrew Christians forgot *the first principles* of their faith. Once they became Christians, their Jewish family members and friends put tremendous pressure on them to return to Judaism and began challenging the basics of the Christian faith. It is clear from this passage that it is impossible to move on toward maturity without carefully understanding the first principles.

This series of booklets is designed to lead you through the first principles so that you can build upon them and grow on toward maturity. In every generation of churches since the time of the New Testament, believers were expected to learn these first principles. In the early church, before new believers were accepted into the church, they needed to learn *the didache* ("the teaching"). "The Didache" was a summary of the basic teaching of the New Testament–the first principles. During the Reformation (1500's), this teaching was called *catechism,* again designed to help Christians master the first principles.

Actually, the concept of *first principles* is important in every area of life. It is central to all quality education. Almost 150 years ago, in the classic work *The Idea of the University,* John Newman referred to a concept he called "pushing up the first principles." According to Newman, the purpose of a university is to teach the first principles of every discipline and then to explore the full limits of those first principles–pushing the principles up through all levels of research.

So it is with our Christian faith. Once we have mastered the first principles, we are able to push them up through all areas of our lives. That is, we are ready to move on to maturity. *The First Principles Series* is carefully designed to help you lay the foundation of your faith.

Whether you are a new believer, a believer who needs to have these first principles laid carefully for the first time, or for whatever reason you need to have them laid afresh, do your work carefully and you will reap a lifetime of benefits.

## The First Principles

### Series I

1. Becoming a Disciple
   *First Principles of the Faith*
2. Belonging to a Family of Families
   *First Principles of Community Life*
3. Participating in the Mission of the Church
   *First Principles of Community Purpose*
4. Cultivating Habits of the Heart
   *First Principles of Disciplined Living*

### Series II

1. Enjoying Your Relationship
   *First Principles of Marriage*
2. Passing on Your Beliefs
   *First Principles of Family Life*
3. Envisioning Fruitful LifeWork
   *First Principles of Ministry*
4. Building for Future Generations
   *First Principles of True Success*

### Series III

1. Handling the Word with Confidence
   *First Principles of Bible Study*
2. Unfolding the Great Commission
   *First Principles from Acts*
3. Laying Solid Foundations in the Gospel
   *First Principles from 1 & 2 Thessalonians*
4. Catching God's Vision for the Church
   *First Principles from Ephesians*
5. Living in God's Household
   *First Principles from the Pastorals*

# Design of the Study Guides

This series is designed to lead you through a learning process–a process designed to teach you to think. This process is based upon the Hebrew wisdom model in the Bible (the Bible's educational literature) and on sound, contemporary, educational research. It is used in all of LearnCorp's Bible studies, so once you have mastered the process it will serve you for all of your future work in these and subsequent series. It will also provide a natural study model that you can apply to all areas of your life.

The first five weeks, you will follow a four-step study process. The sixth week is a summary session and final step. You will "pull together" all of your work from the first five weeks into a final project and share it in your small group.

### Consistent Study Process (CSP)

A Consistent Study Process (CSP) is used in these books to take you through a complete learning cycle every time you study a passage or concept in the Scriptures. CSP can also serve as a convenient reminder that Bible study is not ESP–we are not trying to mystically experience the text, but to carefully and soundly study the text. There are four basic steps to this process and one final step that integrates the work from the first four.

***The First Five Weeks:*** In the first five sessions of every First Principles study guide, the four basic steps will be done each week: 1) Study the Scriptures, 2) Consult the Scholars, 3) Think Through the Issues, and 4) Apply the Principles.

The importance of each step is explained below.

## Study the Scriptures

This step is foundational. We cannot begin exploring the issues of the Bible without first understanding exactly what the passages mean. Discussion groups in which everyone simply shares his opinion are disrespectful of the Scriptures, and therefore to God. They are often merely a pooling of ignorance.

You will go through this same first step in every session, in every booklet. You will begin with a passage to read, answer a few basic questions about the passage, and finally summarize the core teaching of the passage.

**Your work in this step:**

- Read the passage.
- Think through the questions.
- Summarize the core teaching of the passage.

## Consult the Scholars

This step is very important as well, although it is not always highly valued by Christians in our generation. God raises up teachers and scholars to serve in every generation. These teachers can do great harm or great good to churches. We have provided you with some solid, carefully chosen research–in nugget form–to stimulate your thinking. These nuggets of research take two forms. One is a brief commentary on the passage. The other consists of several short instructional quotes on the ideas related to the core truths of the passage.

**Your work in this step:**

- Read and reflect on the brief commentary.
- Read and reflect on the key quotes.
- Record any insights from the readings.

## Think Through the Issues

This step is designed to help you think through the implications of the core teaching of the passage that you have been studying. Unless we go through this process, we can gloss over the significance of the core truths–the first principles of the faith. This is best done in a small group where issues can be discussed thoroughly. Debate an issue in light of the biblical text and try to come to one conclusion as a group. It is not a time for airing opinions but for genuine interaction with the issues.

**Your work in this step:**

- Think through the issue before discussion.
- Record initial thoughts on the issue before discussion.
- Discuss the issue in your small group.
- Record final thoughts after the discussion.

## Apply the Principles

This step brings the basic learning cycle to completion. It is not enough to gain a clear grasp of an issue. It is not enough to accurately understand the core truths of a passage or verse in the Bible. We must apply it to our lives. Applications should be specific and related to the core truths of the passages studied.

**Your work in this step:**

- Think back through the first three steps.
- Design an application for your life.
- Design intergenerational applications

***The Sixth Week:*** The last session in the study guide is the final step.

## Reshaping Our Lives

This step brings together the entire study process. In each of the first five weeks, we moved through the 4-step Consistent Study Process (CSP). Now in the sixth week, you will pull together all of your work and evaluate your whole life.

Too often today, we stop short of what is necessary to really change our lives. Thinking through simple applications is very important as we study the Bible, but thinking through our whole lives in light of these new truths is essential. The final step in the study process requires that we rethink our entire lives in light of the truths we have been studying–that we rearrange our worldview. We must allow the truths to reshape every aspect of our lives.

**Your work in this step:**

- Commit your heart—by reflection, personal journaling, and prayer.
- Commit your mind—by forming clear convictions and memorizing Scripture.
- Commit your life—by decisions, personal projects, and life habits.

***Two Final Parts of the Study Guides:*** Each study booklet contains two additional parts–a glossary and a lifelong learning section.

**Glossary of Key Biblical Terms and Concepts—**The glossary is designed to help you with important terms that you may have encountered for the first time in this study. They are kept to a minimum in the guide, but it is not possible or preferable to remove all terms with special meaning. New terms–especially biblical terms full of rich truths–just have to be learned. To make this process easier, we have included a glossary.

**Lifelong Learning—**This final section introduces you to additional resources that you may want to pursue. After completing this study guide, it is crucial that you do not view yourself as finished. You must understand that you are laying foundations for a lifetime of learning. Several resources are recommended for your further development.

# CULTURAL CONFUSION — MARRIAGE REDEFINED

## SESSION 1

As we mentioned in the introduction, the contemporary family is going through radical redefinition. This redefinition is affecting or will affect almost every culture in the world. The essence of this redefinition is found in the marriage relationship. Not only are roles being radically redefined, but so is the very essence of manhood and womanhood–masculinity and femininity. The effect of all of this is devastating to the local church and, therefore, to carrying out the Great Commission of Jesus Christ. In this session, we will examine the effect on individual families of not following Christ's design for His household, the local church. We have chosen to examine a passage that clearly sets forth the relationship between the guidelines for His household–a family of families–and the stability of individual families. Titus 1:10-16, an often-unknown passage, gives us the key to the relationship between Christ's instructions for individual family units, including marriage, and for His churches and thus for His overall purpose and mission. Those bringing a different teaching were accused by Paul of upsetting whole families. Let's examine this passage carefully to understand why this teaching is so important.

### Study the Scriptures

***Read the Passage:*** Titus 1:10-16

***Think Through the Questions:***

1. What was "upsetting whole families"?
2. What does it mean to be "sound in the faith"?
3. Why did many of the Cretan believers need to be rebuked to be sound in the faith? How had their culture affected them after their conversion?
4. In this context, in what sense were those bringing a different teaching rebellious?

***Summarize the Core Teaching of the Passage:***

Write a paragraph, outline, annotate, or chart your conclusions–whatever best communicates for you. Be sure to comment on the relationship between a different teaching and "upsetting whole families."

Core teaching of Titus 1:10-16:

## Consult the Scholars

The following comments are designed to help you better understand the passage and to stimulate your thinking on the implications of the teaching.

***Read and Reflect on this Brief Commentary on Titus 1:10-16:***

This is a very interesting passage when considered in its context. Remember, Paul wrote to Titus to direct him to complete the process of establishing the new churches that were planted on the island of Crete.

Paul gave him a set of household instructions for the local church family to live by. In the passage immediately preceding our passage, Titus 1:5-9, he instructed Titus to appoint elders in every church. Two specific things (among many others) were to be true of these elders. They were to do a good job leading their own households, and they were to stand firm in the faith, able to exhort and correct those who contradicted it. This leads to Titus 1:10-16, where they had to deal with those who were upsetting the very families they were trying to establish in the faith.

The elders needed to be sound because there were those out there, and even within the churches, who were rebellious. Evidently, in Paul's day, the island of Crete was a rather rough, undisciplined culture. The ethics were bad in the country as well, with little respect shown for authority, honesty, or even law. As we know today, it is possible for whole cultures to become dishonest. The Cretans were becoming known as such a culture. There were some who were preying on the young churches, attempting to get them to stop listening to Paul and his team and to listen to them instead. Evidently, they were after some sort of personal gain. Regardless of their teaching, it contradicted Paul's; consequently, it was upsetting the faith of whole families. Rather than majoring on sound living, sound families, and relationships, as emphasized by Paul in Titus, they were trying to get these families to focus on doctrinal differences, the law, and superstitious myths.

What all is included in "the teaching" (v.9) of Paul and the other apostles? It covers everything written in the letters of Paul and the other apostles that is included in the New Testament. The specific topic at hand is ordering the household of faith. Remember from our studies in *Belonging to a Family of Families,* there is a form of literature called *household texts.* There are two types of household texts—community and immediate family. The context of Titus is a community household text. In other words, it is written for the purpose of instruction on how a local household community, a local church, should be structured. 1 & 2 Timothy are also community household texts. Titus assumes that the principles from the individual household texts, on ordering individual families, are being followed as well. (See *Belonging to a Family of Families.*)

So how does this all tie together? Those who brought another teaching were upsetting whole families. They were either rebellious to the teaching or attempting to contradict it with another teaching. In this context, *sound teaching* means "teaching lived out in the local church community and in the family according to the Master's instructions." Thus any teaching that regards it as outdated, culturally irrelevant, or undermines or contradicts it in any way would be considered as ultimately undermining the establishing process of believers. It is also important to note that the instructions for how we are to live in our families and in the local church family, which are directly referred to as sound teaching, are essential for the progress of the gospel.

Today a new philosophy has entered the church that truly upsets whole families. As mentioned in the introduction, the family itself is being redefined. The instructions of these household texts and the order they establish within individual households and ultimately the household of faith are being undermined at every turn. These instructions are considered outdated. New words are surfacing such as *egalitarian* and *feminism,* and old terms such as *patriarchal* are cast as outdated and controlling. The biblical concepts of *manhood* and *womanhood* are not even addressed. Issues are confused, families are upset and fragmenting, and our churches, in many cases, are all but rendered ineffective!

### *Read and Reflect on Key Quotes:*

The following two quotes are taken from *Recovering Biblical Manhood & Womanhood* edited by John Piper and Wayne Grudem. This book is a compilation of many authors who have carefully written to defend the biblical teaching on marriage and the family, as found in the New Testament. The writers are all part of an outstanding modern day church council called Council for Biblical Manhood and Womanhood. The first quote is by John Piper, who serves as a pastor in Minneapolis and who has written several significant works focusing on God and His work in our lives. It appears in chapter one, "A Vision of Biblical Complementarity: Manhood and Womanhood Defined According to the Bible."

> "The tendency today is to stress the equality of men and women by minimizing the unique significance of our maleness or femaleness. But this depreciation of male and female personhood is a great loss. It is taking a tremendous toll on generations of young men and women who do not know what it means to be a man or a woman. Confusion over the meaning of sexual personhood today is epidemic. The consequence of this confusion is not a happy and free harmony among gender-free persons relating on the basis of abstract competencies. The consequence rather is more divorce, more homosexuality, more sexual abuse, more promiscuity, more social awkwardness, and more emotional distress and suicide that come with the loss of God-given identity.
>
> "It is a remarkable and telling observation that contemporary Christian feminists devote little attention to the definition of masculinity and femininity. Little help is being given to a son's question, 'Dad, What does it mean to be a man and not a woman?' Or a

daughter's question, 'Mom, what does it mean to be a woman and not a man?' A lot of energy is being expended today minimizing the distinctions of manhood and womanhood. But we do not hear very often what manhood and womanhood *should* incline us to do. We are adrift in a sea of confusion over sexual roles. And life is not the better for it....

"The conviction behind this chapter is that the Bible does not leave us in ignorance about the meaning of masculine and feminine personhood. God has not placed in us an all-pervasive and all-conditioning dimension of personhood and then hidden the meaning of our identity from us. He has shown us in Scripture the beauty of manhood and womanhood in complimentary harmony. He has shown us the distortions and even the horrors that sin has made of fallen manhood and womanhood. And he has shown us the way of redemption and healing through Christ.

"To be sure, we 'see through a glass dimly.' Our knowledge is not perfect. We must be ever open to new light. But we are not so adrift as to have nothing to say to our generation about the meaning of manhood and womanhood and its implications for our relationships. Our understanding is that the Bible reveals the nature of masculinity and femininity by describing diverse responsibilities for man and woman while rooting these differing responsibilities in creation, not convention.

"When the Bible teaches that men and women fulfill different roles in relation to each other, charging men with a unique leadership role, it bases this difference not on contemporary cultural norms but on permanent facts of creation. This is seen in 1 Corinthians 11:3-16 (especially vv. 8-9, 14); Ephesians 5:21-33 (especially vv. 31-32); and 1 Timothy 2:11-14 (especially vv. 13-14). In the Bible, differentiated roles for men and women are never traced back to the fall of man and women into sin. Rather, the foundation of this differentiation is traced back to the way things were in Eden before sin warped our relationships. Differentiated roles were corrupted, not created, by the fall. They were created by God."[1]

The second quote is by Elisabeth Elliott, who has served as a missionary in Ecuador where her husband was killed by those whom he was evangelizing. She has written many excellent books on the role of women and developing commitment as Christians. She is truly one of the godliest older women writing today. This quote appears in "The Essence of Femininity: A Personal Perspective," which is also found in *Recovering Biblical Manhood & Womanhood.*

"Feminists are dedicated to the proposition that the difference between men and women is a matter of mere biology. The rest of us recognize a far deeper reality, one that meets us on an altogether different plane from mere anatomical distinctions. It is unfathomable and indefinable, yet men and women have tried ceaselessly to fathom and define it. It is unavoidable and undeniable, yet in the past couple of decades earnest and high-sounding efforts have been made in the name of decency, equality, and fairness, at least to avoid it and, whenever possible, to deny it. I refer, of course, to femininity–a reality of God's design, and God's making, His gift to me and to every woman–and, in a very different way, His gift to men as well. If we really understood what femininity is all about, perhaps the question of roles would take care of itself.

"What I have to say is not validated by my having a graduate degree or a position on the faculty or administration of an institution of higher learning. It comes not from any set of personal tastes and preferences. It is not a deduction from my own genetic leanings or temperament. Instead, it is what I see as the arrangement of the universe and the full harmony and tone of Scripture. This arrangement is a glorious hierarchical order of graduated splendor, beginning with the Trinity, descending through seraphim, cherubim, archangels, angels, men, and all lesser creatures, a mighty universal dance, choreographed for the perfection and fulfillment of each participant.

"For years I have watched with growing dismay, even anguish, what has been happening in our society, in our educational system, in our churches, in our homes, and on the deepest level of personality, as a result of a movement called feminism, a movement that gives a great deal of consideration to something called personhood, but very little to womanhood, and hardly a nod to femininity. Words like *manhood* and *masculinity* have been expunged from our vocabulary, and we have been told in no uncertain terms that we ought to forget about such things, which amount to nothing more than biology, and concentrate on what it means to be 'persons.'

"...Perhaps it should not surprise us that secular higher education has long since discarded the image of femininity as utterly irrelevant to anything that really matters, but it is calamitous when Christian higher education follows suit. This is what is happening. Shortly before he died, Francis Schaeffer said, 'Tell me what the world is saying today, and I'll tell you what the church will be saying seven years from now.'

"It is my observation–and, I may add, my experience–that Christian higher education, trotting happily along in the train of feminist crusaders, is willing and eager to treat the subject of *feminism,* but gags on the word *femininity*. Maybe it regards the subject as trivial or unworthy of academic inquiry. Maybe the real reason is that its basic premise is feminism. Therefore it simply cannot cope with femininity.

"Secular philosophy comes at us daily with terrible force, and we need Paul's admonition to the Roman Christians, 'Don't let the world around you squeeze you into its own mold, but let God remake you so that your whole attitude of mind is changed' (Romans 12:2, *Phillips*). Feminist philosophy, which sounds reasonable enough on the surface, is a subtle and pervasive poison, infecting the minds of Christians and non-Christians alike."[2]

---

Record any insights from the brief commentary and quotes:

## Think Through the Issues

Society today is radically redefining marriage, even to the level of reshaping our understanding of biblical manhood and womanhood. It is easy to begin adopting the ideas of culture without even thinking about them. In fact, anyone who doesn't accept the principles of culture is often regarded as somewhat different, someone who is backwards or out of date. This can put pressure on our marriages and the raising of our children. In this issue, we will examine the implications of building marriages on the first principles of Christ rather than on those of the world around us.

**Issue:** Modern marriages and the first principles

### *Think Through the Issue Before Discussion:*

1. What major influences have shaped your philosophy of marriage?
2. What if you discover that Christ's design for marriage is significantly different from your philosophy? Different from what culture idealizes?
3. Why would Christ even care about how we structure our marriage relationships? How we define our roles and responsibilities?
4. What might be some of the implications of moving a direction that is different from how culture defines the marriage relationship?

---

Record your initial thoughts on the issue before discussion:

***Discuss the issue in your small group.***

Record your final thoughts on the issue after discussion:

## Apply the Principles

It is now time to respond to what you have studied and discussed. Take your time on this section.

***Think Back Through the First Three Steps.***

***Design an Application for Your Life.***

In light of the direction culture is moving, think through your marriage to gain a sense of the degree to which contemporary culture is defining your marriage. Purpose to examine your marriage in light of Christ's design for His household and for the families and marriages that make up His family. As a disciple, reaffirm your commitment to building every phase of your life around the first principles of Christ.

***Design Intergenerational Applications.***

You need to think through these issues whether you are married or not. How can you encourage your children and grandchildren to affirm these principles in their marriages? If you are divorced, how can you affirm Christ's design for marriage in your children? If you are a young adult, you need to affirm this design now so you will build your future marriage on God's design. If you are single, how can you envision using these principles with the people around you—at work, in your neighborhood, in your extended family and church family—to encourage them in their marriages and possibly to give them a glimpse of the Christ that you follow?

---

There are two aspects to the assigned project. First, evaluate the forces that have shaped your philosophy of marriage. Second, reaffirm your commitment to building your mariage, and/or to helping others build their marriages, on the first principles of Christ. Your evaluation and reaffirmation:

# GOD'S BASIC DESIGN FOR MARRIAGE
## SESSION 2

In the midst of all of this cultural confusion, it is absolutely essential that we build a basic framework for our marriages. Once we have a basic framework in place, we can rest confidently in the fact that we will not–as Francis Schaeffer warned–automatically slide into the philosophy of the culture. If you remember from *Belonging to a Family of Families,* the household texts are designed to give us just such a framework for both our families and for the local church family. Without such boundaries, we would quickly become lost in a sea of cultural confusion. In this session, we will build this framework using Ephesians 5:22-33. This passage sets the boundaries for God's design for the marriage relationship. Once it is carefully understood, the entire relationship takes shape and direction. And, we can rest assured that we are laying foundations for lasting relationships that will not only be enjoyable but will produce fruit for generations to come.

## Study the Scriptures

***Read the Passage:*** Ephesians 5:22-33

### *Think Through the Questions:*

1. What are the essential guidelines for the husband in a relationship?
2. What are the essential guidelines for the wife?
3. What is inferred and not inferred in the concept of submission?
4. How does Christ's example, of giving up His life for us, set the boundaries for understanding the love and headship of a husband?

### *Summarize the Core Teaching of the Passage:*

Write a paragraph, outline, annotate, or chart your conclusions–whatever best communicates for you. Be sure to describe the essence of God's design, listing the core responsibilities of both the husband and the wife.

Core teaching of Ephesians 5:22-33:

## Consult the Scholars

The following comments are designed to help you better understand the passage and to stimulate your thinking on the implications of the teaching. This is our third visit to this household text. If you remember from *Belonging to a Family of Families,* session 3, the entire text extends from 5:22-6:9. It gives us God's design for the entire household. In *Cultivating Habits of the Heart,* session 3, we visited the passage a second time, focusing on 6:1-4, guidelines for the habit of training children in the household. Now we will study 5:22-33, where the marriage relationship is the focus.

### *Read and Reflect on this Brief Commentary on Ephesians 5:22-33:*

The basic design for marriage is very simple. This passage lists one main guideline for the wife and one main guideline for the husband. A wife is to respect her husband, the essence of which is to submit to him. The husband is to love his wife, the essence of which is to lay down his life for her. Yet, the passage unpacks each guideline, helping us to get the full implications of each one. Let's look at each one in depth, following the logic of the passage.

First, the guideline for wives. The guideline simply stated is this: Wives respect your husbands. Now what does this mean in its context? The core of the idea is stated in 5:22: "Wives, *be subject* to your own husbands." In the New American Standard Bible, you notice that the phrase "be subject" is in italics. This means that it is inferred in the text, but the actual words are not in the text itself. The words *be subject* appear in 5:21 and 5:24. Some argue that since it states in verse 21 that we are to be subject to each other, that a wife is to be subject to her husband and the husband to his wife. Yet the passage clearly calls for a wife to be subject to her husband, as it does for children to obey their parents. (For a more complete reasoning of this point, see the treatment of this passage in *Belonging to a Family of Families,* page 32.) The word *submission* literally means "to assume a place or position under another person." Synonyms include *subordinate, submit,* and *obey.* It is used in the military for subordinate rank. The standard set forth is Christ and His church (5:24). The church is to be *subject* to Christ in everything, and so the wife to her husband.

The reason that the wife is to submit to her husband is that her husband is the head of the family as Christ is the head of the church, God's household. This is the way God designed things to work. It has nothing to do with the value of one person over the other. Rather, it is just a reflection of God's design—in essence, a reflection of God's wisdom. Paul had previously addressed the Corinthian church concerning this order in 1 Corinthians 11:3. There he states that Christ is the head of man, man is the head of woman, and God is the head of Christ. Is God of greater value than Christ? Of course not! All of this somehow reflects the wisdom of God's design of all things. I am convinced that the more we reflect on this design in the overall context of Christ's plan for His church, the more we will see "the manifold wisdom of God" in full display in our lives (Ephesians 3:8-10).

The essence of this guideline for the wife is summed up in the word *respect,* as found in 5:33. The heart of the submission idea is far more than who makes the final decision if you cannot agree. It is far more than "someone has to lead, God just happened to choose the husband." It is tied to the very essence of manhood and womanhood. *Respect* literally means "to fear" someone. In this case, it doesn't mean being afraid but rather showing reverence as one would towards anyone carrying on an especially important role or responsibility in life. You see, it is not enough to just submit externally, but respect is also part of it. *Respect* reflects an inner attitude or spirit as well. We will develop this concept of respect more fully in our next session when we study 1 Peter 3:1-7.

Second, the guideline for the husband. The guideline simply stated in 5:25 is this: Husbands love your wives. Now again we must ask, what does this mean in its context? Again, the standard set forth is Christ's love for His church. The essence of that love was that He gave Himself up for her–He was willing to die for her. Therefore, the husband must be so committed to his wife that he is willing to die for her. Christ's love for His church was also developmental in nature. He wanted the church to be all that God intended it to be: to fully develop, to completely mature. A husband is to use all of his resources and abilities to help his wife fully mature in Christ. He must not pursue his own spiritual growth independent of his wife's. He is to serve her interests as fully as his own. There is to be no difference. They are truly one.

Paul quotes from Genesis 2:18-25, specifically verse 24, to back up his point. In this context, the woman, who was created from man and brought to him, is to become one flesh with him. The implication of being *one flesh* is that the man is to care for her as he would himself. He is not to view his wife as one of his possessions, but rather as he would himself. Everything is shared. Just as he would seek to grow in Christ and be all that God intends him to be, so he is to love his wife and see that she is cherished and nourished.

As mentioned above, the idea of these roles is tied into the very nature of what it means to be a man and what it means to be a woman. Paul draws on the passage Genesis 2:18-25, which defines man and woman for us. We will examine this concept of man and woman more in the next session. But you can see that more is meant here than just the point, "Someone needs to lead. It just so happens that God chose the man!" It relates in some way to how God created us. The man is not just to lead but to love his wife–to nourish and cherish her. The wife is not just to submit but to respect her husband.

### *Read and Reflect on Key Quotes:*

On two different occasions in Series One of the First Principles Series, we introduced you to the writings of Stephen Clark and his seminal work *Man and Woman in Christ.* We will refer to this work several times in this booklet on marriage and in the next one on raising children. Here Clark comments on Ephesians 5:22-33:

"The 'household code' in Ephesians (and Colossians) then, does not teach on everything which goes into the relationships it considers. Rather, this part contains a very specific kind of exhortation, an exhortation on order in those relationships. The household code follows a statement (Eph 5:21) that says, 'Because you fear Christ, subordinate yourselves to one another.' Paul then develops this statement by exhorting wives to be subordinate to their husbands, children to obey their parents, and slaves to obey their masters. Each of these exhortations has a complementary exhortation to husbands to love their wives, to fathers to avoid provoking their children, and to masters to treat their slaves well. In other words, the whole passage from Eph 5:21 to 6:9 (likewise Col 3:18-4:1) treats subordination in several relationships among people who make up the same household. Paul directs his primary attention to the subordinates in the relationships, urging them to subordinate themselves to those who are over them. He then urges the 'heads' to behave in such a way toward the subordinates that they can be peacefully and gladly subordinate. Thus the passages on husbands and wives in the household codes concern one aspect of relationships in the household—the aspect of order (subordination). This perspective gives us a key to reading Eph 5:22-33....

"Subordination in the Christian community is not simply a human affair, a matter of convenience or wisdom. Christ stands behind it, because he is concerned for the good order which makes his body functional (Col 2:5). The husband has authority over his wife not simply because of nature and not simply because of some social custom, but because Christ has delegated that authority to him, so that when the wife subordinates herself to him, she is obeying Christ. The husband is the representative of Christ. This does not mean that the wife should relate only to Christ and regard her husband as the medium or occasion for her obeying Christ. Paul is trying to create a relationship of subordination between people, and he is encouraging her to subordinate herself to her husband. His instruction is not 'subordinate yourself to the Lord and pretend that your husband is the Lord.' His exhortation is rather 'subordinate yourself *to your husband,* because of the Lord.' The husband is a human being, but he bears the Lord's authority in this relationship. Thus, Paul takes what could be a natural subordination and situates it within the order of the Christian community, an order that Christ stands behind.

"To understand this passage and its teaching about order in the husband-wife relationship in the Christian community, first the exhortation to the husband, and then the exhortation to the wife will be considered. The husband is exhorted to love his wife. Paul is not here talking about erotic love, sexual desire–the love of contemporary popular songs. The exhortation does not mean 'husbands, desire your wives.' The love that Paul speaks of here is service-love, the love Christ has as he cares for the church, the love he had when he laid down his life on the cross. That Paul means service-love and not erotic love can be presumed from the general New Testament use of the word 'love' (*agapē, agapaō*) and also from both the context and content of the passage....

"The wife, correspondingly, is exhorted to subordinate herself to her husband (5:21-22). The subordination that Paul urges here stems from the unity of the husband and wife in the family, a point which the comparison with Christ and the church makes particularly clear. The purpose of the subordination is to provide a deeper and more solid oneness between husband and wife as they function together in the household. The Greek term translated 'subordination' (*hypostassō*) has a military use that makes a helpful comparison. It was used to describe an ordered army or a fleet drawn up in battle array, ready to function together as a unit. According to the New Testament, something similar should be true of husbands and wives. Their subordination has a practical aspect in that it creates a greater effectiveness in their working together as one."[3]

---

Record any insights from the brief commentary and quotes:

## Think Through the Issues

We live in a culture where the roles of men and women and husbands and wives are in a state of almost total confusion. The biblical design, based upon Christ's plan for His church, is either twisted to accommodate our contemporary lifestyle desires or is simply not understood, for lack of serious study of the Word. It is critical that we learn to think clearly and biblically about the essence of God's design for marriage.

**Issue:** God's basic design for marriage

***Think Through the Issue Before Discussion:***

1. If we desire to build our marriages on the household instructions in Ephesians, what pressures would this cultural confusion bring on us?
2. What does it really mean to follow these guidelines? How far should we take them?
3. What is the logic of the way Christ set up Christian marriages? How does the design appear to fit with Christ's overall plan for His church?
4. In what way will these guidelines lead to stable, lasting marriages?

Record your initial thoughts on the issue before discussion:

***Discuss the issue in your small group.***

Record your final thoughts on the issue after discussion:

## Apply the Principles

It is now time to respond to what you have studied and discussed. Take your time on this section.

***Think Back Through the First Three Steps.***

***Design an Application for Your Life.***

The application of this session is focused on how your marriage lines up with the biblical guidelines found in Ephesians 5. Reflect on the state of your marriage. Are you following these guidelines? Is your marriage in line with Christ's design? If not, where do you need to make changes? Are they major?

### ***Design Intergenerational Applications.***

You need to think through these issues whether you are married or not. How can you encourage your children and grandchildren to build their marriages according to these guidelines? Are you reinforcing them as you converse with your sons and daughters? If you are divorced, how can you teach Christ's design for marriage to your children? If you are single (young or not), what changes do you need to make in your idea of how a marriage relationship should work, for your future and to encourage others?

---

Record your thoughts on how you need to adjust your marriage — or your ideas concerning marriage — to align more closely with Christ's design:

# SPIRIT OF A MARRIAGE
## SESSION 3

In session two, we worked on building a framework for the marriage relationship that is according to God's design. We built this framework out of one of Paul's household texts–Ephesians 5:22-33. In this session, we are going to study another one of these household texts, this one by Peter–1 Peter 3:1-7. Together these two passages form a rather complete picture of what God desires for His disciples as they live together in marriage. While following the same basic design, Peter focuses on the spirit of the marriage. This passage gives us a more intimate look into the very heart of God's design for relationships. It shows the beauty of the proper spirit of a wife towards her husband and a husband towards his wife. It is easy to focus on the external elements of God's design and miss the internal response that He is looking for. This passage truly gets to the heart of the matter.

## Study the Scriptures

***Read The Passage:*** 1 Peter 3:1-7

### *Think Through the Questions:*

1. What is the essential internal quality that God is looking for in a wife toward her husband?
2. What is the essential internal quality expected of a husband toward his wife?
3. In what sense is a wife a "weaker vessel"?
4. What do prayers have to do with the spirit of a marriage?

### *Summarize the Core Teaching of the Passage:*

Write a paragraph, outline, annotate, or chart your conclusions–whatever best communicates for you. Be sure to describe the essential internal quality of wives and of husbands and the relationship of those qualities to their prayers.

Core teaching of 1 Peter 3:1-7:

## Consult the Scholars

The following comments are designed to help you better understand the passage and to stimulate your thinking on the implications of the teaching.

***Read and Reflect on this Brief Commentary on 1 Peter 3:1-7:***

This is the other major New Testament passage on marriage. It too is a household text. Though teaching the same essential design for marriage as Paul (Ephesians 5:22-33), Peter gives significant additional insights. Together these two passages give a rather complete picture of God's design for marriage, as well as its intended beauty.

Peter wrote to churches who were experiencing persecution for their faith, reminding them of their calling and their hope and challenging them to remain faithful. This passage appears in the context of exhortations to honor those who are in authority in their lives even if they are unreasonable. This is also alluded to in the beginning of the passage where he encourages wives to be submissive to their husbands even if they are disobedient to the word–possibly meaning they are not believers.

In this passage, 1 Peter 3:1-7, Peter sets forth the same basic guidelines that Paul did in the Ephesians text we studied last session. In both passages, wives are to be submissive to their husbands. Peter, however, gives us much more insight into the spirit of the marriage relationship. He calls the wife to put on a "gentle and quiet spirit," and he focuses the husband on the importance of honoring his wife. Let's look first, at the directives to wives.

Peter reaffirms the core responsibility of wives to be submissive to their husbands. Rather than building on Christ's role as head of the church, he focuses on Christ's own example of submissiveness when mistreated. The point is to be submissive even if the husband is not following the Lord. The key to being able to do this is found in a phrase in 3:5, where it says that Sarah "hoped in God." If God is real, then there is nothing to fear in a disobedient husband, for He is in control. The inference is that the situation will enable God to work in a special way in the husband, winning him to obedience. The specific thing that will win him is the spirit that is at the heart of the wife's submission. She needs to be respectful, as was emphasized by Paul in his passage. But here, Peter peers even deeper into Christ's design for the marriage. At the heart of respectful submission is a "gentle and quiet spirit," 3:4. *Gentle* refers to one who is considerate and unassuming. One who has a *quiet spirit* is one who is calm and at ease. Note in the passage, she is even respectful in how she addresses him.

The directive for husbands is more internal as well. They are to live "in an understanding way." The term for *understanding* is one that refers to "a personal and growing knowledge," a knowledge probably based both upon the first principles of Christ and on a personal knowledge of one's wife. He then uses two terms that, if not carefully reflected upon, may be offensive to some who have adopted our culture's definition of women. He refers to women as *weaker vessels*. It is most likely that he is emphasizing what we all know about men and women–that men are generally stronger and more aggressive. Women are generally weaker physically and more sensitive as well. This is backed up by the phrase "since she is a woman." Those words, *woman* and *man,* return our thoughts to the passage Paul quoted from in his marriage text–Genesis 2:18-25. In 2:23 it sates "she shall be called Woman, because she was taken out of Man." The very heart of the definition of the Hebrew word for *woman* is "soft," for *man,* it is "strong." Before our cultural revolution redefined manhood and womanhood, these differences were obvious. In light of the differences between men and women, Peter calls the husband to a high level of sensitivity. The husband should also lead the relationship with real knowledge, which only grows out of the first principles of Christ. And, he is to honor his wife–esteem her as having enormous worth–since she is an equal heir of life in Christ. Only then will their prayers as a household and for their household be fully realized. In other words, failure to live in marriage according to the first principles of Christ will hinder the effectiveness of a household in the service of the Lord as He seeks to build His church.

It is now time to readdress the issue of biblical manhood and womanhood, which is also part of the essence of the directives given to husbands and wives in these household texts. It is clear that there is a difference between men and women, and men are to lead their wives with great sensitivity to these differences. Women are to develop beautiful internal spirits toward their husbands. Men are to lead, provide, protect, nurture, and to possess a love that is so strong that it makes their wives' interests as central as their own, even to the point of laying down their lives for them. This is what a husband is to look like, and it defines the very essence of manhood. Wives are to respect, follow, and honor their husbands. They are to develop a spirit toward them that does not challenge their direction but is gentle and at ease, based on a confident trust in God; in addition, a spirit that is always seeking to please them. They must orient their lives towards their husbands and speak respectfully to them and of them. Aspects of womanhood are seen in these directives as well.

### *Read and Reflect on Key Quotes:*

Again, Stephen Clark is especially helpful in gaining an accurate understanding of men and women in Christ in his comments on 1 Peter 3:1-7:

> "Although 'subordination' primarily describes a way of relating to another person, it also involves a character trait, a disposition to respond in a certain way. Subordination extends beyond obedience to commands to also include respectfulness and receptiveness to direction. 'Submissiveness' is probably the best English term in such contexts. 'Submissiveness,' in this sense, is an overall character trait

related to humility which all Christians should possess. The Christian character is portrayed in scripture as respectful of authority, not rebellious. Men as well as women should be submissive in their subordinate relationships. However, 1 Peter 3 especially urges wives to be submissive in their relationship with their husbands. They are to have a respectful and quiet spirit, qualities which derive from their fear of and trust in the Lord. The passage says that a wife's quietness and peacefulness are rooted in her acceptance of God's order for her life and a trust in him. The wife can be submissive because she knows that God stands behind Christian order, and he cares for her, either through her husband or sometimes in spite of her husband.

"The final verse of the passage, the exhortation to the husbands, contains a great deal of important material. A more literal translation would read as follows: 'Likewise you husbands, live with your wives according to knowledge, bestowing honor on the woman as the weaker vessel, since you are joint-heirs of the grace of life, in order that your prayers may not be hindered.' The 'knowledge' referred to here is undoubtedly the knowledge of God. Husbands should live with their wives according to God's revelation.

"Then the passage exhorts the husbands to take concern for their wives. As in Ephesians 5, the wives are first urged to subordinate themselves to their husbands, then the husbands are urged to behave toward their wives in a corresponding way, a way which expresses the proper functioning of their role. In Ephesians, husbands are urged to care for their wives. In 1 Peter they are urged to honor them. Scripture sees both care and honor as appropriate for the relationship and as qualities that make subordination easier for the subordinate, allowing the head to rule more effectively. The husband is urged to explicitly express his wife's value and importance. Since some may construe subordination to mean being of less value, the husband should take care to express his esteem for his wife. Moreover as he, the head of the house, expresses his esteem for her and as he takes care to establish her in her position as the second authority in the house, the others in the household will be drawn to a greater respect for her. If her husband treats her with honor, she will gain respect through her subordination rather than lose it. One of the more important tasks of the father in a family is to treat all the household members in such a way that they gain respect. He is, in fact, the one in the best position to create respect for his wife and children."[4]

Record any insights from the brief commentary and quotes:

## Think Through the Issues

It is possible to understand Christ's design for marriage and yet to miss the very heart of His design. Christ has established order in the household for many reasons as He seeks to build His church. One of the reasons is to create beautiful marriages that reflect the beauty of God's wisdom for all to see. In order to grasp the full intention of God's design, reflect on the inner elements of Christ's design and contrast its essence with that of contemporary culture.

**Issue:** Spirit of a marriage

### *Think Through the Issue Before Discussion:*

1. In what way is it possible for a wife to submit to her husband externally and yet miss the real internal elements of God's design?
2. In what way is it possible for a husband to lead and yet really miss the whole point of his responsibility?
3. How would you define the spirit of God's design for the marriage relationship?
4. How can you see these guidelines building true emotional love and bonds in a marriage relationship?

---

Record your initial thoughts on the issue before discussion:

***Discuss the issue in your small group.***

Record your final thoughts on the issue after discussion:

## Apply the Principles

It is now time to respond to what you have studied and discussed. Take your time on this section.

***Think Back Through the First Three Steps.***

***Design an Application for Your Life.***

In this section you probed deeper into Christ's design for marriage, looking at the very heart, or spirit, of that design. How is the spirit of your marriage? Do you, as a wife, have a gentle and quiet spirit toward your husband? Do you, as a husband, live sensitively with your wife, as one who understands God's design for women, for marriage, and for the purpose of your family? Evaluate the heart of your marriage in light of Christ's design.

***Design Intergenerational Applications.***

As a single adult or young adult, think about the spirit of your relationships with the opposite sex. What is your spirit towards them? How does it line up with Christ's design? Evaluate how you think you would do in marriage? What do you need to work on now to lay good foundations for the future? If you are an older single or widow, how can you encourage those in the church who need to embrace the significance of these truths? If you are divorced, work on your own inner response—first to please the Lord, then as a model for your children, and finally, maybe God will use your change to put you back together with your spouse, if that is still possible.

---

Evaluate the heart of your marriage in light of Christ's design, and record your thoughts on what it would take to build that kind of marriage:

---

# MARRIAGE & COMMUNITY LIFE
## SESSION 4

In sessions two and three, we focused on building a framework for the marriage relationship. We built it out of Paul's and Peter's household texts, both of which gave us the core ingredients of God's design for the relationship. It is one thing to understand the basic biblical design; it is another thing to carefully build your marriage around these principles. You may never have had any good models. You may have years of marital conflict to overcome. You may have been building your marriage upon the spirit of the culture, and the roles may feel or seem unnatural. Regardless of your situation, we can all benefit from the assistance of mature couples who have made it work. Remember, we are all part of a local church family, not just an immediate family. This is part of God's design–to give us the support we need over the long haul to build solid marriages. In this passage, we will look at the importance of getting "training," from those who are mature, in building lasting and enjoyable marriages and in living responsibly by Christ's principles within the local church family.

## Study the Scriptures

***Read The Passage:*** Titus 2:3-5

### *Think Through The Questions:*

1. What is the role of older women with younger women?
2. What are they to teach the younger women?
3. Why is it important for younger wives to love their husbands and to build solid relationships?
4. In what way does a good marriage depend on vital involvement in community life?

### *Summarize the Core Teaching of the Passage:*

Write a paragraph, outline, annotate, or chart your conclusions–whatever best communicates for you. Comment on the role of older women teaching younger women, why it is important in building strong marriages, and why strong marriages are important to the local church community.

Core teaching of Titus 2:3-5:

## Consult the Scholars

The following comments are designed to help you better understand the passage and to stimulate your thinking on the implications of the teaching.

### *Read and Reflect on this Brief Commentary on Titus 2:3-5:*

This passage again sends us back to the basic directives that Paul gave to Titus, who was responsible to fully establish the churches. There is an order, a way of doing things, in the community life of the household of God. This order is there to help us focus on the things we really need to be majoring on in the lives of our churches. It is easy to get focused on the wrong things, things that feed our anxieties and distract us from the real matters of faith–things such as building strong churches, building strong families that produce mature children in the faith, and establishing churches that are a base for penetrating nations and communities beyond with the gospel.

In Titus 2, Paul urged Titus to exhort the older men, older women, younger women, and younger men in how to live so that their lives would best adorn the gospel in the community in which they lived. Our passage at hand, Titus 2:3-5, is found in this context. Specifically, he encouraged the older women to teach the younger women. What were they to teach them? The basics of a solid marriage and family life. Why was that the core content of what they were to teach? Because strong families are central to the effective witness of a local church in its community! Paul was reasoning from the framework of producing strong churches on the island of Crete, but the same applies to us today.

Let's look specifically at some of the instructions. They were to teach the younger women to love their husbands and children. The word for *teach* is interesting here. It means "to train someone in sound thinking or living." Its root is literally *wisdom*. So the idea is for older women to impart wisdom, based upon the teaching (first principles), to the younger women in how to build strong marriages, sound relationships with their children, and solid family lives. It is also interesting that they were to train the younger women to love their husbands and children. *Love* here is the word for affection and caring. Evidently, this is something that can be lost over time, and it is also something that can be developed or cultivated. Loving affection and care for a husband are something to be trained in–this is a totally different message from infatuation and the romantically driven image of love portrayed by our culture. (Though not addressed in this passage, a caring and affectionate sexual relationship is also part of cultivating this love for one's husband, as with the husband toward his wife. See I Cor. 7:3-6.) Also, notice again the idea of being subject. And finally, "workers at home," which does not mean that outside enterprises are beyond the scope of a wife's sphere (See Proverbs 31 where the wife was a real entrepreneur.) but that caring for and nurturing a solid home and marriage is the central task of a young wife.

Today these instructions are used to back up large teaching ministries of women who are oftentimes not even truly older women. That is not the purpose of this passage. Husbands are responsible for teaching their families, including the full development of their wives (Ephesians 5:22-6:4). Elders and ministers of the gospel, such as Timothy, are responsible for the instruction and preservation of sound doctrine in the local church family that they lead. Older women are to help younger women live soundly in that teaching, especially within their own households. This opens the door to a tremendous ministry for older women and emphasizes the centrality of the household for young wives.

Today in this culture, we need tremendous reinforcement for our young wives. Just think of the pressures on them. On one hand, they are to develop a whole career and a completely successful identity in the world around them. In the church, they are to build solid homes and ministries. If they focus on their marriage and home, they are culturally out of step and often suffer from identity issues. If they try to do both, they burn out. There is a tremendous need for older, mature women to come alongside younger women and to help them think biblically about their responsibilities in the home. The key here is mature, older women. Often today, it seems that there are few truly godly, older women who have loved their husbands, raised committed children, and are able to share true wisdom–real answers. Often instead, we have merely a sharing of failures and the giving of permission to continue to fail.

This passage infers directives for young husbands as well. Marriage is not easy; it takes cultivation. It takes the life of a community. We should not put unrealistic pressures on our wives to produce a lot of money for the family. We must lead our wives by nurturing an environment for them to be all that God intended for them. We must truly value their work on behalf of the household. We must be committed to the local church community, and to our own families, and especially to our relationships with them. We must resist the pull to focus our lives around work, neglecting the foundations of our homes and marriages. In this passage, older women are to teach younger women, but this does not exclude older men from teaching younger men. It just focuses on the very central role of wives in building households of faith, including enjoyable, loving marriages.

### ***Read and Reflect on Key Quotes:***

Today we focus on the nuclear family (husband, wife, and children) not on the extended family (grandparents, aunts, uncles, etc.) or on the function of that family in a larger believing family–the local church community. Everything centers on the emotional bond of the marriage relationship itself. Yet, this is not the biblical way of thinking. A marriage relationship is fully enjoyed in the context of true community. Anything else places demands on the relationship that were never intended in God's design. Just as we cannot live as individuals without community, we cannot live as nuclear families isolated from true community (what Clark calls the "nuclear family approach") and function as fully, according to God's design. Again, Stephen Clark speaks right to the issue in his book *Man and Woman in Christ.*

"Secondly, important structural elements of family life—such as subordination, commitment, and complementary roles for men and women—must be restored in order to strengthen family relationships. These elements must be restored in an effective way, however, or they will fail to bring the strength needed for family life. The 'Christian nuclear family approach' tends to give husband and wife identical roles and has them do many things together and hence works against some of these essential elements. Advocates of such strategies often speak of the importance of man-woman complementarity, but in such a relationship husband-wife 'complementarity' comes to mean one of two things: (1) the interaction of the different personalities and gifts of the husband and wife (the same kind of complementarity that could exist between two men or two women, or that could exist in a functional situation), or (2) the interaction of the male personality and the female personality which occurs when the two are doing the same things together. This latter approach to complementarity tends to strengthen the emotional dependence between the man and woman in marriage, but weakens the true interdependence, because each is not depending upon the other to take the primary responsibility for different aspects of their common life. If the man is not there, the woman can do everything just as well, and vice versa. On the other hand, 'complementarity' in the early Christian pattern (and in most, if not all, human societies of the past) meant that the husband and wife had different spheres of responsibility which they fulfilled separately, but with the woman subordinate to the man. This type of complementarity is one which greatly strengthens family life.

"Finally, in strengthening the social structure of family life, the modern competition between the nuclear family and the broader Christian community must be broken, and the nuclear family must be placed within a larger social context that supports, rather than opposes, the family and its relationships. The 'Christian nuclear family approach,' in reinforcing that competition, poses a major obstacle to what is most needed for strengthening family life. The larger Christian social system is just as crucial as the smaller family unit when it comes to strengthening family life. Along these same lines, the men of the Christian community should take responsibility for community life. They should, however, assume this broader responsibility in a way that strengthens the family. They need to act as the representatives—the heads—of their families, overseeing their families' involvement in the wider community and representing their families' needs to the wider community. In some significant way they need to bring their sons with them so that their sons can be trained as Christian men and are not separated from their fathers. The men need to experience their responsibility as heads of their families so that they can be attentive to the real needs of their families. In short, the role of the men is the main structural link between the smaller unit of the family and the larger unit of the community. Simultaneously restoring the men's sense of responsibility for both family and community is a key piece in the strengthening of family life, both internally and in its relationship to a larger social grouping."[5]

Record any insights from the brief commentary and quotes:

## Think Through the Issues

Our individualism in Western culture carries on over to our marriages and families in ways of which we are unaware. We tend to think that strong, enjoyable marriages are based upon lots of individual, emotional time together rather than on building solid family units within true community. We also tend to think that our marriages, and especially feelings of love, are just there and do not need to be built or cultivated. Moreover, we think we can sort it all out ourselves, without the aid of mature older men and women to mentor us.

**Issue:** Importance of community life to a solid marriage

### *Think Through the Issue Before Discussion:*

1. What is the role of older men and women in helping build strong, enjoyable marriages?
2. How does the idea of being trained in the marriage and family basics of Titus 2:4-5 square with our contemporary ideas of love, intimacy, and romance?
3. What does it mean to learn to love your husband? Wife?
4. How important is true community in building a truly enjoyable and meaningful marriage?

---

Record your initial thoughts on the issue before discussion:

---

***Discuss the issue in your small group.***

Record your final thoughts on the issue after discussion:

## Apply the Principles

It is now time to respond to what you have studied and discussed. Take your time on this section.

***Think Back Through the First Three Steps.***

***Design an Application for Your Life.***

In the space provided below, write out your conviction on the importance of true community in building strong marriage relationships. Affirm your commitment to being fully involved in the life of a community of believers. If you are young, think through older women or older men whom you could look to, to give you wisdom.

### *Design Intergenerational Applications.*

Regardless of your age, think through the importance of true community in building strong marriages. Affirm your commitment to true community. Record both. If you are older and have, or have had, a solid relationship, make a commitment to assist younger women and men in their marriages. If you are young, seek out older women and men who have really succeeded in their marriages to give you insight and advice.

---

Your convictions on the importance of true community in building strong marriages, and people you plan to seek out:

# BUILDING AN INTERGENERATIONAL COMMITMENT

## SESSION 5

God's design for marriage involves far more than just building enjoyable relationships. As we saw in session four, building strong relationships requires the mentoring of older, mature believers. We also saw the importance of strong marriages to the life and witness of the local church community. In this session, we will continue to develop an understanding of Christ's first principles for marriage by focusing on the end of the marriage relationship. From this, we will again see why marriage is so critical, both for the life of the believing community and for the spiritual heritage of our children. In this session, we will study a passage that focuses on widows, those who have lost their mates. From it we can learn much about the intergenerational element of marriage. You will see that part of *enjoying your relationship* involves the intergenerational heritage that is produced by it.

## Study the Scriptures

***Read The Passage:*** 1 Timothy 5:1-16

### *Think Through The Questions:*

1. What do we learn about the marriage relationship from the guidelines given to and concerning widows?
2. From this passage, what can we learn about some of the intergenerational purposes of marriage?
3. Why did Paul want younger widows to get married?
4. Why is being "the wife of one man" so important? (See also 1 Timothy 3:2 and Titus 1:6.)

### *Summarize the Core Teaching of the Passage:*

Write a paragraph, outline, annotate, or chart your conclusions–whatever best communicates for you. Be sure to record your observations on the permanence and intergenerational elements of marriage.

Core teaching of I Timothy 5:1-16:

## Consult the Scholars

The following comments are designed to help you better understand the passage and to stimulate your thinking on the implications of the teaching.

### *Read and Reflect on this Brief Commentary on 1 Timothy 5:1-16:*

This passage is in the large household section of Paul's letter to Timothy, which describes how believers should live within the household of God. It focuses on the issue of widows. In it, we see some very important insights into how we are to think about both the permanence and the intergenerational elements of marriage. In this world that focuses marriage on the short-term goals of personal satisfaction and sexual fulfillment, we usually fail to see the whole, integrated picture of our lives. However, from the vantagepoint of widowhood, we can see the full intent and the full significance of the marriage relationship.

The passage begins with a reminder that as believers we are to live as if we are a family. Timothy was to treat everyone as family: older men as fathers, younger women as sisters, etc. At one level this is a picture of what it means to live in a local church community–to live as a family. But, it is more than just an illustration. We really are an extended family. This is seen by the guidelines surrounding how to deal with widows in the church family.

The basic principle is this: Each family is to care for its own widowed parents, yet, if individual families who are part of the church family cannot care for them, then the church family is to care for them. You see, the church is a real family. Individual families still exist, yet we are also a large family with very real obligations to each other. This is part of Christ's administration (1 Timothy 3:14-16) and, therefore, part of what it means to be a disciple.

How does this all relate to the marriage relationship? First, look at the ideal widow in 1 Timothy 5:9-10, whom the church would consider supporting because of her service to the church family. What does it say about her? She has a reputation for good works. This is key and is mentioned in several ways. She has served the church, using her home as a base. Notice, it also says that she has been "the wife of one man." This is one of the qualifications for elders who serve in the leadership of the church family as well. 1 Timothy 3:2 and Titus 1:6 state that elders need to be "the husband of one wife." The same is true of deacons in 1 Timothy 3:12. Why is this always emphasized for ideal roles within the church family? One reason is that a permanent marriage relationship is needed to bring about a strong, intergenerational aspect to the family and the church family. If the church is a family of families, then the families of the church must have permanent marriage relationships at their base. This is part of Paul's argument in 1 Corinthians 7:12-16, where he encouraged a believer to remain married to an unbeliever for the sake of the witness of the unbelieving spouse and for the sake of the children, who would still be under the umbrella of one believing parent. The ideal then, without exception, is remaining married to one person for life. There is a permanence and an intergenerational element to marriage.

Let's relate this back to building an enjoyable marriage relationship. In our culture, we focus on the needs of the individual. We look at the marriage relationship primarily from the vantagepoint of getting our needs met. We have endless how-to books on developing intimacy, on communication, and sexual skill. We also have a prevailing belief in our culture, backed up by endless books and an entire counseling profession, that encourages us to get out of marriages that have lost their love and become merely functional relationships. It is even argued that this will be better for the children in the long run. Yet, a review of the literature produced in the wake of this philosophy, such as *Fatherless America* by David Blankenhorn, will show the utter devastation that comes from such a philosophy. It is clearly not the philosophy (first principles) of Christ. Christ's philosophy calls for permanent commitments to marriage, as far as it depends on us. It calls us to see our relationships in light of strengthening Christ's church and fulfilling the great commission. It calls us to see the intergenerational elements of permanent marriage relationships in the lives of our children. It recognizes that many will need to learn to fully love their husbands, wives, and children and that love is something that can be cultivated and grown. It recognizes that true enjoyment is made up of more than just personal needs being met in a relationship. It recognizes that true enjoyment in marriage is based on things that count for eternity–building a heritage to further God's purposes. These principles will be unfolded in the next three books of this series, leading to the building of a solid, intergenerational heritage.

It is true that intimacy, good communication, companionship, and even romantic love (including cottage vacations alone for enjoying each other's love in the autumn season of marriage, see the Song of Solomon) are part of God's design. But, they are not the whole picture, not the foundation of true joy. We will deal with communication, intimacy, and romantic love in the *LifeSkills Series–The 4th Generation Series,* which follows the *First Principles Series.* Yet, it is important to remember that though these things greatly enhance the enjoyment of a relationship, the foundation of all true joy comes from fully serving God and His purposes.

### ***Read and Reflect on Key Quotes:***

The following quote is by Edith Schaeffer, the wife of Francis Schaeffer. It is taken from her book *Common Sense Christian Living.* Edith has written a whole series of excellent books on the home and family, building a complimentary body of literature to her husband's comprehensive works on building a Christian worldview. Her works are rich and insightful. In this quote, she reflects on the importance of permanent, lasting relationships, which span several generations.

> "When we hear statistics of the ratio of divorces to marriages, we must realize that many, many people have never been part of relationships that last a long time. Children are growing up in an atmosphere in which temporary relationships are the 'normal' way of life.

The dividing of a child's time between 'a weekend with father' and 'weekdays with mother' is more confusing than simply the broken unity of the together names 'Mother and Father.' The breaking up of the name 'Mom and Dad, which is a couplet that spells solidity, a solid home to which to return after physical or mental travel, is confusion enough. But the confusion is compounded when the short weekend with father includes another woman whom the child is supposed to 'relate to, Dear.' And the multiplication of confusion comes in the man that now has taken Father's place with Mother, and the added grandparents, sisters, and brothers who have *no* blood ties, and new babies that are half-brothers or half-sisters. No wonder a little boy of seven in such a situation sighed deeply and exclaimed, 'I can't wait until I grow up and can have a home of my own!'

"Why is it that relationships are being gloomily regarded as something that can not ever go on and on? Is it a twisted understanding of what a human being is capable of? Is it a lack of knowing that there is *anything* in the universe that continues? Is it a loss of observing any two people or a family working at the upheavals that come day after day in their living under the same roof with a feeling that there is something worth working for?

"The capability of human beings having lasting relationships that span several generations has been shoved aside, not believed possible, not prepared for, not expected to be demonstrated! Relationships that go on through unpleasant incidents–disagreements of a variety of sorts, difficulties big and little, hurt feelings, unfair treatment of each other, unthoughtfulness, forgetfulness, silence and lack of communication for a period, moods, and sudden anger–are considered to be archaic, old-fashioned and something to be scorned...not something that can be worked on and improved.

"There is an oft-repeated statement these days: 'Children are better off if their parents divorce because a home where there are fights and constant disagreements is very bad for them.' Period!

"What is ignored all too often is the fact that children discuss with other children the signs of an impending divorce and what terrifies them, and brings tears in the night, is the fear that the fights they are overhearing mean a split is on its way. No one of any age feels comfortable when people are shouting at each other, but there is a measure of comfort in being assured that although this disagreement may *sound* fierce, there *will* be a solution. One of the two who are arguing will have enough imagination and ingenuity to work out a solution concerning the day off or the vacation about which there is such a difference of opinion! Is the soup burned? A resourceful cook will hurry and make a substitute without continuing the argument that, 'it can't be tasted.' Children need to see *solutions* take place, not only as a reassuring factor in their present home lives, but as an example for the future.

"Children need to be able to say to other children, 'Well, my mother and dad get a little upset at times. One or the other gets very angry at other times. But they do love each other really, and they love us, and they have lots of imagination and many ideas as to how to make it all up and do something pleasant together after the fight is over!' Sadly, very few children today have seen the pattern of living *through* differences, coming out the other side of them, of someone's apologizing to someone else–or both apologizing–and then one of the two having a brainstorm about going for a picnic, eating supper in front of the fire, having watermelon out under the lilac bushes, playing a game after supper, reading two chapters of the current book while nibbling on popcorn, or getting out a map and planning a 'someday kind of a vacation.' And very, *very* few children have friends who can tell them how it works!"[6]

---

Record any insights from the brief commentary and quotes:

## Think Through the Issues

Our culture has lost the value of long-term relationships that keep future generations in the forefront. Our marriages have become focused on meeting the needs of the marriage partners over building a heritage for the future. This has affected Christian families deeply. Our steady diet of how-to books on intimacy, communication, and relational skills has created a self-focus rather than challenging long-term commitments driven by the goals of building strong churches and an intergenerational heritage dedicated to serving God's purposes.

**Issue:** Intergenerational marriage commitment

### *Think Through the Issue Before Discussion:*

1. What are some of the reasons you see for the tremendous focus on intimacy, communication, and relational how-to books in Christian bookstores?
2. In what way does making a permanent, lifelong commitment to marriage–where divorce is not an option–lay a foundation for a truly enjoyable relationship?
3. In what way do solid, intergenerational marriages further Christ's purposes in building His church? In fulfilling the great commission?
4. What all, do you think, goes into building a lifelong marriage?

---

Record your initial thoughts on the issue before discussion:

***Discuss the issue in your small group.***

Record your final thoughts on the issue after discussion:

## Apply the Principles

It is now time to respond to what you have studied and discussed. Take your time on this section.

***Think Back Through the First Three Steps.***

***Design an Application for Your Life.***

In the space provided below, write your initial thoughts on what all is involved in building a permanent, lifelong marital relationship. List any changes that would be needed in your attitude and life in either making or renewing such a commitment. Reaffirm your lifelong commitment to your husband or wife.

***Design Intergenerational Applications***

If you are divorced, think through the impact of your broken relationship on your future heritage and share you convictions (especially if newly formed from this study) with your children. Talk with them about the importance of these truths with the view of laying new, inter-generational guidelines for the future. If not married, think through the idea of being permanently married and record your convictions and thoughts and why these convictions are important for you to have. If older or widowed, think through how to communicate these truths to your children or grandchildren (or others), and begin praying for them.

---

Your convictions on the importance of permanent, lifelong marriages—both to the local church family and to the development of a future generation committed to serving the Lord—and your thoughts on what it would take to build that kind of marriage:

---

# RESHAPING OUR LIVES
## SESSION 6

We now have a fairly complete picture of the first principles governing the marriage relationship. These principles give us a framework for building enjoyable, lasting marriages—marriages that will not only be rich and rewarding but will contribute significantly to the church for generations to come. All this is quite a contrast to the culture around, where we find marriages and families breaking apart at an alarming rate.

It is now time to pull together all of our applications from the first five sessions, in order to affect our whole lives. In this fast-paced world, it is hard to find time to do any serious reflection. While we have benefited from the exercises in the first five sessions, actually integrating the truths into our lives as a whole takes extra effort. Taken together, they can become a powerful force bringing about significant change—change designed to reshape our lives.

### Committing Your Heart

**Reflection, Personal Journaling, and Prayer**

Journaling is an excellent way of reflecting more deeply about the significance of what we have been learning. It forces us to express in words what has entered our hearts. It helps us identify and clarify what the Spirit has been using in the Word to enlighten our hearts, as well as to convict us. Prayer should follow this. We should ask God to permanently transform our hearts to give us a desire and longing to grow to maturity.

In this section, think back over your work from each of the five previous sessions. What happened in your life because of your work in each session? Record your thoughts, and reflect on what you wrote. What new convictions have you developed? What have you seen God begin to do in your life? Are there areas that you wish you had followed through on more fully? What affected you most? What convicted you most? What excited you most? How has your philosophy of marriage changed?

Finally, formulate these thoughts into one main prayer request. If you were to ask God to help you (or others) build this kind of satisfying, lasting marriage, how would you ask it? Write the request in a paragraph. Transfer it to a 3 x 5-inch card and carry it with you. Pray over it regularly. Over the next few weeks, record, on the back of the card, any ways that you see God answering your prayer.

---

Your Journal — thoughts on building (or encouraging others in building) an enjoyable and lasting marriage:

---

Prayer Request:

---

# Committing Your Mind

## Forming Clear Convictions and Memorizing Scripture

It is essential that we pull together what we have studied–formulating our thoughts into clear convictions. What is Christ's design for marriage? What are the first principles of building a marriage? And, what is your role as a husband or a wife? It is critical that we think clearly about the truths of Scripture. If we have wrong ideas in our heads, then our marriages will be built on those wrong foundations. If we misunderstand Christ's design for marriage, it can greatly affect the future generations of our families as well as the stability of the local church community. If we follow our own plan instead of Christ's, our marriages and families are at risk.

Begin by summarizing your studies concerning building an enjoyable, lasting marriage into one paragraph–ideally bringing together all of the key truths that you have studied in the five sessions. Then, list the essential Bible references to back up your convictions. Finally, choose at least one of these verses to memorize, record it below, and quote it by memory to your study group when you meet. Transfer it to a 3 x 5 inch card–writing the verse(s) and reference on one side and your insights into the verse(s) on the other side. Review it for about 6 weeks.

---

Building an enjoyable and lasting marriage—core convictions:

Key verse to memorize:

## Committing Your Life

### Decisions, Personal Projects, and Life Habits

Think back over the "Apply the Principles" section of each of the five sessions. It is one thing to think about specific applications to our lives as we move through each study. It is another thing to think across our whole lives and begin reshaping our life goals and lifestyles by what we are learning. This is a vital part of building a satisfying and lasting marriage. Several things are necessary in order to integrate these principles into our lives. First, look back over your "Apply the Principles" sections and your work so far in this session. Are there decisions that you need to make? For example, do you need to rethink your philosophy of marriage? How is the spirit of your marriage? Are you faithfully fulfilling your roles and responsibilities in your marriage? Do you have any older role models and mentors in the church? Are you encouraging others in their marriages? What kind of overall adjustments do you need to make in your life direction as a result of this study?

Decisions, personal projects, and life habits:

# Glossary of Key Biblical Terms and Concepts

The following is a list of important terms that you may have encountered for the first time in this study. Although they are explained in the booklet, it is easy to forget their exact meanings. This glossary can also serve as a catalogue of biblical terms and concepts for future reference.

**Egalitarian.** A contemporary term used to refer to the idea that all things should be decided equally, on a 50/50 basis, rather than one individual or group being entrusted with the decision-making responsibility. The term is particularly used by some Christians who argue against men leading in their marriages and homes.

**Femininity and Masculinity.** Terms used today to identify the essence of what it means to be a man and a woman. The term *feminine* represents a series of traits common to females and *masculine* represents a series of traits common to men. Today, in a distorted attempt to make all things equal, our culture destroys these differences. Scripture sees basic differences in men and women that are worked out in different roles and responsibilities in marriage, family, and the church family.

**Feminism.** A movement, now worldwide, that began in the early 1900's to attempt to bring about total equality of men and women, even to the extent of radically de-emphasizing the naturally observed differences of men and women. There has been special emphasis on equal roles and responsibilities for women in the home and workplace. A movement has developed among some Christians that is called *biblical feminism.*

**Headship.** A concept developed in several of Paul's letters. Again, it has to do with *order* in Christ's administration. Christ is the head of man, man is the head of woman, and God is the head of Christ (1 Corinthians 11:3). It has nothing to do with value, unless you conclude that Christ is of less value than God. In Paul's marriage text (Ephesians 5:22-33), the husband is to be the head, or leader, of the family. Today, some have tried to redefine *head* as "source," which distorts the context and stretches the possible meaning of the word.

**Intergenerational Heritage.** A term used in this book to focus on the idea that a significant part of the marriage relationship was designed by Christ to produce a strong family, from which will come generations of committed believers.

**Manhood and Womanhood.** Terms used today to identify the essence of what it means to be a man or a woman. It is obvious from 1 Peter 3:7, that the term *woman* carries some different ideas than *man*. In Genesis 2:18-25, Eve is called "Woman, because she was taken out of Man." The Hebrew word for *woman* carries the idea of "soft," and the word *man* carries the idea of "strong."

**Nulear family.** Stephen Clark refers to this concept in his quote in session four. This term refers to a Christian approach to the family that recognizes the value of the family over our Western culture's idolizing of individualism, but it fails to see the family as part of a Christian local church community. The family becomes the center, replacing the centrality of the local church community.

**Patriarchal.** A term used for men leading their families and especially extended families, or family of families. Abraham, for example, was a patriarch. Some cultures have set up patriarchal structures that are oppressive to women and children. As a result, some Christians have taken this reality to be the biblical model–which has nothing to do with biblical headship and male leadership–to promote their egalitarian and feminist ideas.

**Postmodern / Postenlightenment.** The new era that is emerging after the scientific age of the last 400 years. Mankind is concluding that modern discoveries and scientific knowledge cannot provide all of the answers to life. There is a spiritual side to life, thus, the era is postmodern. Today, when a marriage is referred to as *postmodern,* it often means that it is an enlightened marriage, based on a redefined idea of family. It is egalitarian in nature, and it is free to be defined however the members want to define it.

**Puritanical.** Commonly used today for anything that is old fashioned, legalistic, or overly strict. Some compare it to anyone who believes in the biblical roles and responsibilities as set forth in the household texts (Ephesians 5:22-33, Colossians 3:18,19 and 1 Peter 3:1-7). The term came from the Puritans, the last group of believers in church history to fully and seriously follow the guidelines of the household texts. This shows how far our culture has removed itself from any order in family life.

**Submission.** A key word in both Peter's and Paul's household texts (Ephesians 5:22-33; 1 Peter 3:1-7). Wives are to submit to their husbands. This does not mean that the wife is of less value than the husband is, for they are equal heirs in Christ (1 Peter 3:7). It is an issue of divine order in the household. The husband is to be the head of the family and represent the family in the church family.

**Weaker Vessel.** Used by Peter in 1 Peter 3:7. It most likely refers to the woman as being physically weaker than the man, as well as being more delicate and sensitive. It builds off the idea that she is a *woman,* which in Hebrew carries the idea of "soft." See Manhood and Womanhood.

# Lifelong Learning

The booklets in this series are designed to lay the very essential foundations of the faith. They are intended to be just a beginning. The writer of the New Testament letter, Hebrews, reminds us that we are to move on to maturity (Hebrews 5:11-14). This "Lifelong Learning" section is at the end of every First Principles Series booklet. It will serve as a guide to some of the resources that will enable you to build solidly on the foundations laid in each booklet and, therefore, urge you to press on toward maturity. Review these resources and include any that you would like to read or work through in the "Committing Your Life" section of the sixth session.

1. ***Passing On Your Beliefs*, The First Principles Series II—Book Two**

   *Passing on Your Beliefs* continues the work done in this booklet by moving the focus to the raising of children. This booklet helps guide you in discovering the biblical principles for raising mature children who continue on in the faith. It goes further than just raising "good kids" but guides you in laying lasting foundations of faith in your children. The four booklets of Series II are all designed to help you build a solid household unit.

2. ***Becoming Established in Your Marriage*, The Establishing Series II—Book One**

   Book one of The Establishing Series II is an advanced version of this booklet. The five units of the course parallel the five sessions of this booklet. Many of the articles quoted in the "Key Quotes" of this booklet are included in full in the course, providing a mini-reader. It is an excellent tool for studying in depth the areas you have begun in this booklet. The course is not yet complete; the target date for release is September 1999. (LearnCorp produces The Establishing Series for BILD-International. To order, call BILD-International at 1-515-292-7012.)

3. ***Recovery of Biblical Manhood and Womanhood: A Response to Evangelical Feminism*, edited by John Piper and Wayne Grudem (Crossway Books, 1991)**

   This is a fairly extensive and difficult text dealing with the whole issue of biblical manhood and womanhood. It is produced by The Council for Biblical Manhood and Womanhood for the specific purpose of dealing in depth with all of the false teaching constantly coming at the churches and "upsetting whole families" (Titus 1:11). It also sets forth solid, biblical answers to many contemporary issues involving biblical roles for men and women in the home and in the church. The two most important articles in the book are:

- "A Vision of Biblical Complementarity: Manhood and Womanhood Defined According to the Bible," chapter 1 by John Piper
- "The Church as Family: Why Male Leadership in the Family Requires Male Leadership in the Church," chapter 13 by Vern Poythress.

Piper's chapter is included in *Becoming Established in Your Marriage,* the Establishing Series II–Book One.

4. ***Man and Woman in Christ: An Examination of the Roles of Men and Women in Light of Scripture and the Social Sciences,* by Stephen B. Clark (Servant, 1980)**

   This text is an extensive treatment of men's and women's roles in the Scriptures. It is over 700 pages. Even though difficult to read, it is the best treatment available. The key chapters are included in *Becoming Established in Your Marriage,* the Establishing Series II–Book One. Clark's book is currently out of print.

---

# *Endnotes*

1 John Piper, "A Vision of Biblical Complementarity: Manhood and Womanhood Defined According to the Bible," in John Piper and Wayne Grudem (ed.), *Recovering Biblical Manhood & Womanhood,* (Wheaton: Crossway Books, 1991), pp. 33, 35. Used by permission of the publisher.

2 Elisabeth Elliot, "The Essence of Femininity: A Personal Perspective," in John Piper and Wayne Grudem (ed.), *Recovering Biblical Manhood & Womanhood,* (Wheaton: Crossway Books, 1991), pp. 394, 395, 396. Used by permission of the publisher.

3 Stephen B. Clark, *Man and Woman in Christ: An Examination of the Roles of Men and Women in Light of Scripture and the Social Sciences,* (Ann Arbor: Servant Books, 1990), pp. 74, 79-80, 81. Used by permission of the author.

4 Ibid., pp. 92-93.

5 Ibid., pp. 622-623.

6 Edith Schaeffer, *Common Sense Christian Living,* (Grand Rapids: Baker Book House Company, 1983), pp. 68-69. Used by permission of the publisher.

# Church-Based Theological Education

As we approach and cross into the next millennium, numerous Western church leaders are pondering the question of how the church will adapt to the rapid cultural shifts swirling through an increasingly global society. While church leaders, religious philosophers, and postmodern theologians analyze the waning of the Western church paradigm, a network of leaders across the globe are establishing believers in the faith and are building strong, reproductive local churches.

How can a former Hindu pastoring converts in his home church in India, a bilingual son of missionaries starting a new work in Québec, a Nigerian charged with training thousands of pastors throughout his nation, and the pastor of a large church in the heart of Silicon Valley possibly have anything in common? They all embrace and are implementing church-based theological education (C-BTE). By implementing C-BTE, the pastor in India has found that he can advance his own study while continuing to pastor his church and prepare elders. The church-planter in Québec has found that he can establish believers in the faith and train the next generation of leaders. The Nigerian church leader has found a way to train large numbers of existing pastors to meet skyrocketing church growth. The pastor in Silicon Valley has found a way to re-establish an existing church and promote like-mindedness across a large ministry team. They all have taken responsibility for leadership training, not relegating it solely to institutions. They all realize that theological education is not just for those who have chosen professional ministry, but for each and every believer.

They have something else in common too, they all are using materials developed by LearnCorp Resources and its sister orginization, BILD-International. *The First Principles Series* is only one segment of an extensive array of comprehensive materials developed for church-based training. From small group Bible study guides to intensive doctoral level currciulum, LearnCorp and BILD have a wealth of materials, seminars, and ministry tools that can benefit any church that is serious about establishing believers in the faith and raising up leadership that is in line with New Testament biblical principles.

To find out more about what LearnCorp and BILD can offer, contact:


**LearnCorp Resources**
P.O. Box 1427
Ames, Iowa 50014-1427
(515) 292-6810 (voice)
(515) 292-1933 (fax)
learncorp@ames.net (email)
http://www.learncorplc.com

**BILD-International**
P.O. Box 1507
Ames, Iowa 50014-1507
(515) 292-7012 (voice)
(515) 292-1933 (fax)
bild@ames.net (email)
http://www.bild.org